I0487479

WHAT LUCY TAUGHT US

*A management fable about improving
your business, one process at a time.*

WALTER GEER

Copyright © 2009 by Walter T. Geer, Jr.
All rights reserved
Printed in the United States of America

All rights reserved, including the right of reproduction
in whole or in part in any form.

ISBN:1-4392-4321-2
ISBN - 13: 9781439243213

Visit www.booksurge.com to order more copies.

CONTENTS

Acknowledgments

No book is ever the product of one person's efforts and, certainly, this was no exception. It would never have become reality without the help and advice of many supportive friends and colleagues. My biggest thanks go to David Alkins, Dr. Milton Samuels, Roscoe Morris, and the staff at The CA Group. Thanks also to Adrienne and Gail, whose editorial corrections and helpful suggestions were invaluable; Sandy Shalton and the publishing team at BookSurge; and finally a "special" thank-you to my wife, Wanda, for being so patient with my late nights. I want to thank her for her ideas, suggestions, and faithful support of my writing this book.

Introduction

In addition to being one of America's most beloved comedians, Lucille Ball was a cultural icon. Her ability to make us laugh was a gift that has withstood the test of time. Along with Ricky, Ethel, and Fred, Lucy taught us to appreciate the importance of friendship and to embrace the humor in our everyday lives. In addition to keeping us laughing, each episode of *I Love Lucy* included at its core an important overriding message.

In the now classic "Job Switching" episode, Lucy and Ethel take jobs wrapping candy on an assembly line while Ricky and Fred tackle the household chores. It's a hilarious episode that reminds us not only to appreciate the work we do (whether at home or in the workplace), but also underscores the importance of *process* in the workplace. Its famous scene of Lucy and Ethel frantically wrapping candy (and missing quite a few!) resonates even more today as businesses struggle with productivity, efficiency, and the need to do more with less. People will always be the primary means for getting things done in an organization. Technology can help, but the employee, supervisor, and manager ultimately define and control how efficiently the work gets done. Or so we've been led to believe.

In my experience with businesses of all types and sizes, management ignores the importance of *process* when searching for answers to "how can we be more efficient?" or "how can we accomplish more with less?" The typical management approach to these questions usually involves playing musical chairs with resources, adding more duties to an already overburdened staff, or changing business requirements. At the end of the day, efforts that fail to respond to these approaches are by and large blamed on the employees involved.

As Lucy showed us, it is *process* and not the employee that drives efficiency and, ultimately, it's how work gets done in an organization. Dysfunctional processes lead to dysfunctional employees—not the other way around. Organizations that have experienced this "aha" moment fully understand the importance of well-designed and well-managed processes.

How, then, does this transformation in thinking occur? In working with a variety of clients over the years, it's become apparent to me that the concept of a business "process" is something that exists solely as a "this is how we do it" mentality, rather than a systematic way to understand how work gets done. Processes exist in our heads. Ask an employee how a particular task is performed and, typically, you'll get *his or her interpretation* of the process. Not surprisingly, that interpretation will vary from person to person. It's rare to find a business process described in the form of a document or diagram. Businesses simply don't see the value in doing this. What they fail to understand is that *documenting* a process allows them to bring their stakeholders to the table to collaboratively confirm and agree upon "the way things *are* done." Once they achieve that understanding, stakeholders can then go about the task of evaluating "how things *should be* done." This mentality can help you achieve tremendous gains in workforce productivity. This becomes enormously important today in light of the economic challenges facing organizations of all types and sizes.

In order to understand the importance of what Lucy taught us and how it can be applied to your environment, I've written a story in the context of a fictional company. The story describes how a simple eight-step strategy can dramatically improve your business processes. I based these concepts on my work with businesses, large and small, in the public and private sectors, and colleges and universities. I've summarized these steps in more detail in a separate section following the story.

The Fable

A New Challenge

Barely a week had passed before the reality of the new job and the big changes in his life began to start sinking in for Joe. The downtime between his former and his new jobs had given him a chance to clear his mind. He was leaving behind the frustrations he'd experienced at Star Manufacturing in return for the prospect of a new, more challenging opportunity at Advanced Medical Devices Inc. (AMD). Making a career change at age fifty was a big risk, but the opportunity was too good to pass up. With Star's management in transition due to downsizing, the timing made sense. Although his job at Star had been secure, Joe had become complacent and bored after ten years in the same department. At AMD, he would have an opportunity to revive an organization with great potential. Because AMD was a much smaller organization, he might also have the opportunity to make a greater impact on the bottom line and, thus, have a higher profile within upper management. He was also excited about the aggressiveness of AMD's management team and their commitment to turn things around. Finally, there was, of course, the attraction of more money. With relatively flat sales over the last two years, getting a substantial raise at Star was simply out of the question. So the move made sense. The only downside he could foresee would be relocating his family at a time when the real estate market was strug-gling. Moving from a small Midwestern town to New England would not only be a financial challenge, but a lifestyle change as well. Nonetheless, his wife, Cathy, fully supported the move and looked forward to this new phase of their life.

Advanced Medical Devices

Advanced Medical Devices was a leading manufacturer of radiation protection products. Medical and dental labs extensively used its radiation shields because occupational exposure to radiation was an ongoing problem for both patients and staff. Started during the high-tech boom of the 1980s, AMD built its success upon innovative products driven by strong research and development (R&D) and attention to customer needs. AMD enjoyed years of double-digit growth before foreign competition began an aggressive move into its domestic market. In order to avoid losing its customer base, AMD began to seek ways to produce its products cheaper and faster. This quest to achieve competitive pricing, however, came at a cost: shipping delays, higher defect rates, and increased customer complaints. To make matters worse, tightening federal regulations regarding radiation exposure had prompted a costly redesign of AMD's entire product line. They rushed new items into production in an effort to respond to these regulatory changes.

Joe was well aware of the challenges in accepting the position of vice president of Operations. By the time AMD contacted him for his first interview, he had researched AMD's sales history, analyzed its product line, and studied its competition. In accepting the job, he had negotiated a hands-off strategy with the CEO that, he felt, would enable him to quickly implement any changes he deemed necessary. His strategy was simple: reestablish customer confidence by understanding customers' concerns and needs, and then delivering on those needs by improving product quality, reducing delivery times, and strengthening customer support. By studying the competition and establishing a "competitive advantage," Joe hoped to distinguish AMD from its competition and reestablish its dominance in the market.

The first order of business would involve meeting with his management team to listen to their thoughts, ideas, and perspectives on the current situation facing AMD.

The Meeting

By the time Joe entered the conference room, Nancy and Arnold had already arrived. He was running a few minutes late that morning. Navigating a busy expressway system each day was quite a change from the ten-minute commute he had enjoyed for years.

As the director of Production, Nancy Hodge had advanced through the ranks at AMD, having started as an inventory clerk twenty-two years ago. A conservatively dressed older woman, her appearance was in stark contrast to her younger colleague, Arnold Boyd. Arnold was a recent MBA graduate from a local college who had managed the Customer Support operation for just over a year now. Dressed in jeans and sneakers, Arnold presented a more relaxed, contemporary demeanor.

The two sat next to each other in the cramped conference room, which until recently had served as a storage room. Maintaining its "start-up" mentality, AMD embraced a no-frills policy that eschewed the types of furnishings typically afforded senior executives.

Joe had met the team before, briefly during one of his interviews. Still, the body language of the two conveyed a slight uneasiness at this first real meeting with their new boss. He was sure by now that they were not only familiar with his background but that they also may have heard through the grapevine what his intentions were for the department. He broke the awkward silence by introducing himself.

"Good morning. I'd like to start by saying that regardless of what you've probably heard, I don't intend to fire anyone—at least not today." The remark appeared to elicit a rather strange reaction from the managers. After uncomfortable moment of silence, he reassured them with a big grin that he was simply kidding. That seemed to break the ice, and he got a light chuckle from them.

"I know there's been a lot of speculation and misconceptions floating around concerning my role as head of Operations. I felt it was important to get everyone together this morning, on my first official day, to hear candidly from me. As I'm sure you are aware, we've got a tremendous challenge ahead of us. We've lost considerable market share in the last two years and our reputation in the industry has suffered. In the meantime, our competition has introduced new products that we still have in development."

Just as he was about to continue, in walked an elderly man carrying a large leather briefcase under one arm. Protruding from the top of the partially open briefcase was a stack of folders. In his other hand, he carried what appeared to be an oversized calculator. With an unshaven beard, a vastly receding hairline, and wire-framed glasses he personified the stereotypical "mad scientist" image.

"Sorry for being late," he said, extending his hand.

"You must be Kurt Linqst from R&D," said Joe, acknowledging the handshake. "We're just starting."

"Get used to it," Arnold said jokingly. "He's never on time for anything."

Kurt took a seat at the opposite end of the table. He plopped the briefcase down on the table as Joe continued. "In order to survive, AMD needs to get back on track quickly. We need to get cost competitive products to market faster and with fewer defects. We also need to get back to one of our core strengths-innovation-by developing products that are better and lighter than that of the competition."

He explained that his first order of business would be to establish a vision for AMD that would guide their new strategy. It came as no surprise to the group that the key to this strategy, in Joe's view, would be improving quality, reducing their development cycles, and strengthening customer support. Heads around the table nodded in agreement.

Arnold was the first to join in the conversation. "I agree that vision and strategy are important. But, how do we get senior management to buy into that?"

"By tying the vision and strategy to our strategic goals," Joe responded. "I don't anticipate that being a problem. In fact, I think our biggest challenge will be *implementing* the strategy. We need to honestly assess our capabilities to understand what effect they have on our ability to get the job done."

Unfortunately, they had all heard this before. "We've had a revolving door of consultants lead us through that activity over the last six months," said Arnold.

"That's right," Nancy added. "I think we have a clear understanding of our issues. What we lack is a realistic plan to address those issues."

"Which are?" Joe asked bluntly.

Kurt broke his silence while searching through the files he had pulled from his briefcase. He appeared to be looking for a specific document. He spoke slowly, emphasizing each word. "In my case, its resources," he answered while peering over his wire-framed glasses that had slid down his nose. "I've been asked to produce more, with less staff. There's simply no way we can get new products quickly through development and into the market at our current staffing level. We're being pushed to reduce the cycle even more, and we have. But management needs to understand that this impacts quality and our ability to support the product adequately."

"Just look at the number of new hires in the sales force," added Nancy. "It's ridiculous. Seems to me, we're putting our resources in the wrong place. Our quality issues are putting a tremendous strain on my rework operation."

"Sure, we're all struggling with staffing issues. That's not going to change anytime soon," explained Arnold, avoiding eye contact with Nancy and Kurt. "As managers, that's our challenge to solve. Our real problem is communication. I'm being left out of the loop in the development process. How can we be asked to effectively support a product if we're not involved in the development and testing cycles?"

Kurt, looking somewhat relieved, finally appeared to locate the document he had been searching for. He tossed it across the table in Arnold's direction. "We've invited you on several occasions to attend our design meetings. Your people simply don't participate, so don't point the finger at us."

"But it's always after the design has been finalized," snapped Arnold.

Joe, sensing the rising tension in the room, decided it was time to table this discussion and move on, leaving these issues for another time.

"The objective of this meeting today is simply so that I could share my plans going forward with you. We'll have plenty of time to address other issues later. In the meantime, I need to understand the entire process from the ground up. In order to do that, I'll need to spend time with each of you and your staff in your respective areas. That'll help me get a better feel for some of the issues you've raised."

"Are you planning to spend time with all operations staff?" Nancy asked, appearing somewhat skeptical of the approach.

"As much as I possibly can. In addition to being able to see every aspect of the operation, it's important that I get to know line staff. Their feedback and suggestions can be very helpful. This'll begin sometime later this week. Are there any more questions?"

No one asked any further questions. At that point, Joe took the opportunity to talk about team values, expectations, and goals. He spent the rest of the meeting sharing his work philosophy, while they listened attentively and took notes. He had given this speech numerous times at Star.

He adjourned the meeting and asked that they block out time in their schedules for him to get a tour of their areas and to meet their staff. Kurt quickly stuffed the stack of folders back into his briefcase and left, followed closely behind by Nancy. Arnold remained seated at the conference table. He appeared somewhat subdued.

"I'm sorry, Joe, if I came off as a little aggressive. I guess I'm the new kid on the block here and I'm not as devoted to the 'old way of doing things' as Kurt and Nancy are," he explained.

"How so?"

"In my opinion, this company appears to be stuck in the past. The way we're organized, how decisions are made, hiring, I could go on for days," he explained. "More than anything, however, the business model is outdated and needs to change. It may have served us well ten years ago, but it doesn't work in today's world."

Joe could sense his frustrations and, to a certain extent, agreed with Arnold's assessment of AMD.

"Coming from a similar environment, I can certainly identify with your concerns, Arnold. Changing the way a business operates isn't an overnight process. In the short term, we need to focus our attention on those things that *can* be changed. Hopefully, that'll include some of your concerns."

Although Arnold appeared to accept this explanation, Joe knew it would be a matter of time before the younger man's patience with the organization might wear thin again. On the other hand, the kid might prove to be an important advocate for his plans for change.

House Hunting

A muffled ring from his phone appeared to come from somewhere beneath the mounds of paper on Joe's desk. It was probably Cathy calling to remind him of their outing at noon. A succession of meetings and interruptions had distracted him and he had lost track of time. As he searched frantically for his BlackBerry, he questioned his need for yet another electronic toy. He finally found the phone but by the time he remembered how to activate the call, the ringing had stopped. Just as he had thought, it was Cathy. Quickly scrolling through his e-mail, he found the message he was looking for.

> *Hi Joe,*
> *Hope you and Cathy are getting accustomed to the big city. Delores has arranged to take you and Cathy through several neighborhoods tomorrow. Let's get together later this week. Let me know when you're free.*
>
> *Bob*

Delores was the name he was looking for. Bob Garcia was an old college buddy who lived nearby. Having a friend in the area to help transition to a new environment had been a key factor in his decision to accept the job. Bob had arranged for his wife, Delores, a real estate agent, to show Joe and Cathy properties in the area. It had been awhile since they last met and, unfortunately, he had forgotten her name. Her company, Lyons Properties, was perhaps the largest real estate company in the Northeast. With a roster of over three hundred full-time sales agents, they covered virtually every city and town north of Connecticut. The current economic downturn had created a buyer's market, so there would be plenty of homes to choose from. Having to buy while still attempting to sell their current home, however, could present a problem in the longer run. In any event, they were looking forward to a new home, a new neighborhood, and the opportunity to meet new friends.

On his way out of the office, he stopped long enough to e-mail himself a copy of AMD's third quarter earnings report to review at home later that evening. Those numbers would be important to review prior to his meeting next week with Harry Davidson, AMD's CEO. He expected Harry to focus on earnings, and more specifically, what Joe's plans were, and how they might affect sales in the short term.

He grabbed his coat, took one last sip of his coffee that had long since gone cold, and informed Amy on the way out that he would be gone for a few hours.

Learning the Ropes

Production was by far the largest department in the operation. It alone accounted for approximately thirty employees working in shipping and receiving, testing, assembly, engineering, and rework offices.

Nancy's office was located on the second floor of the five-story building, right across from the Billing Department. The physical location of her office made it difficult for her to monitor her production process that occupied virtually the entire first floor.

It was a small office. A mixture of AMD service awards and pictures of her family covered the walls. She had been a widow for several years now and, as a result, had become deeply committed to her job. Twelve-hour days were normal for her. On the wall above her desk hung a framed motivational poster—*Teamwork: Common people attaining uncommon results.* Both the picture and the caption were familiar to Joe.

"Sorry," Nancy explained as she came through the door. "Had a small issue to resolve, down in the assembly area. I hope you haven't been waiting too long."

"No. As a matter of fact, I just got here myself."

"So," she said, sitting down in her office chair looking somewhat exhausted, "where would you like to start?"

"First, how about a quick walk through the entire production process? Then I'd like to start my tour of duty in the rework area."

"Any particular reason for starting with rework?" she asked.

"It interacts with just about every part of the business," he explained. It's also an area where we really need to contain costs."

As they walked through each area, Nancy made it a point to introduce Joe to each staff person. He met an interesting mixture of young college grads and older, more conservative types who had likely been around since the company's earliest days. Most seemed friendly and somewhat curious about their new boss whose plans had not yet filtered down to their level. The operation was much larger in scale than any he had managed before.

Rework

The area supervisor met Nancy and Joe as they approached the rework area. In all, Nancy had five lead supervisory reports. "I'd like you to meet Charlotte Ortiz, our rework supervisor," said Nancy.

"Hello, Joe. Glad to finally meet you," she said, removing her goggles and lab coat. "Please excuse my appearance. I've been down in the shop area all day. It gets a little dirty down there."

"I understand you've got quite an operation here," said Joe.

"We interact with just about every part of the business here. I think it's a good place for you to start," she said.

Nancy was scheduled to be in a conference call with a supplier shortly so she decided to leave the two of them to continue the tour.

Charlotte led Joe toward the back of the shop, just past the loading docks to an office area of cubicles. In front of the cubicle area was an office with a large window overlooking the entire area. As they entered the office, Joe noticed that she had the same motivational poster behind her desk as Nancy.

"I see you share Nancy's philosophy on teamwork."

"You'll see that in every office here," she said with a smile. "It was an effort by your predecessor to inspire a team approach here at AMD."

"And...?"

"We've had a long history of working as a collection of independent operations. To a certain extent, it's worked for us. To suddenly change that was asking too much of the staff here."

Joe was both curious and concerned.

"So working together is a problem here?"

"I wouldn't call it a problem. We get things done, but sometimes the way we interact does tend to get in the way. Personally, I think that'll be one of your biggest challenges here."

"Within Operations?"

"Not only Operations, but working with other areas also, like Sales."

That was important to know. It was certainly an unexpected addition to his growing list of concerns. He had assumed rebuilding AMD would involve some "people issues," but now it appeared as if he would have to address issues outside of his responsibility as well. At some point, he'd have to get back to that discussion but right now he needed to focus on the rework operation. He was curious to know how all the pieces fit together.

"Everything starts with the customer," she began. "We work closely with customers to understand their specific needs. Kurt and his R&D group are responsible for developing the actual product design. Once R&D finalizes the design, Engineering develops the specifications needed to manufacture each component in the design. Third-party vendors then manufacture the components and ship them to us based upon our assembly schedule."

"So we receive the parts just-in-time for production?

"That's the idea, but it never seems to work the way it should for a couple of reasons. First of all, we extensively test all incoming parts for compliance to the specs and requirements."

"And that's done by the Testing Department?"

"That's right," she continued. "If a part's not in compliance with the spec, we create an Exception Report and submit that to R&D. They determine if the noncompliance issue is minor enough to waive, or if the component should be rejected and returned to the vendor. If the latter happens, our assembly schedule is affected."

"And the vendor makes a strong case for a waiver, rather than scrap the shipment," said Joe.

"Of course."

He was beginning to get the picture.

"From our perspective, however, a noncompliant issue could affect customer safety. That could turn into a big liability for us."

"And what about the components that pass inspection?" asked Joe.

"They get tagged as AP, or, 'acceptable for production.' They stay in storage until scheduled for assembly. Once assembled, each product goes through a final inspection before it's moved to our shipping department for delivery to the customer."

"So there's no manufacturing on site?"

"That's right. We're basically an assembly shop."

The process seemed rather straightforward to Joe. "So how does rework come into play?"

"Government regulations that control radiation exposure levels are constantly changing. That means having to retrofit a lot of our existing products in the field to meet compliance. It's part of our service commitment to our customers."

"Instead of reworking existing products why not give them incentives to purchase new products that comply?"

"That happens in some cases. But remember, many of our installed products are unique. We just don't have the capacity to fill new orders and make replacements at the same time."

Joe nodded his head. "Another resource issue," he said to himself. He'd heard that quite a few times this week.

He thanked Charlotte for taking the time to give him a quick overview and reiterated his desire to spend time in each of the areas to get a hands-on view of the process. That way, he could get a slightly different perspective by talking directly with those actually involved in the day-to-day tasks.

Harry

A month had passed now and this was only the second time Joe had met with Harry. He was sure Harry would press for quick answers and solutions. Although he had a good sense of the issues by now, some unanswered questions still remained.

Harry Davidson was one of the founders of AMD. He had steered the company through both the struggling start-up years and the high-growth years. With the loss of significant market share, his leadership had come under fire. The company's failure to acknowledge both a maturing market and the threat of foreign competition had become a point of contention with the board. To make matters worse, AMD had taken advantage of its market dominance by refusing to adjust its pricing structure in a struggling economy.

Harry was in the middle of a phone call with a customer when Joe arrived. "I'll just be a second longer," he whispered while motioning for Joe to come in and sit down. His large, imposing figure hovered over the small desk.

"Damn it, Frank, that's ridiculous," he said, raising his eyebrows at Joe as if to imply that the person on the other end was crazy. He paused before continuing. "What can we do to make this work?" He listened attentively to the response. "I understand. I'll get back to you later today," he said, his voice dropping as he hung up the phone.

He placed his glasses next to the phone and exhaled while loosening his tie. Joe could sense a more serious problem lurking below the surface.

"You've seen the third quarter sales figures. We're barely keeping our heads above water. The foreign competition is killing us. It's been a tough year and we sure as hell can't afford to lose this contract. We need to push the sales team harder while finding ways to cut costs out of the product. It's as simple as that."

"We've seen a lot of new activity in R&D recently," added Joe.

"I'm aware of that, but very little has actually resulted in new business," Harry grumbled. "The sales team is focusing on a potential opportunity in South America right now that looks promising. In the meantime, I need you to focus on getting our cost down. At this point, nothing's off limits."

"There are a couple of issues that we can address right away. Take a look at this," he said, handing Harry a report. "I had Nancy pull this together."

Harry reached for his glasses.

"We're averaging about four to five production delays a month. The average delay is two weeks. For some reason, it appears we've been receiving an increasing number of non-compliant parts from our vendors. That's killing our delivery schedule."

"So, lean on the vendors. If that doesn't work, find someone else who can do the job right," Harry snapped.

"I'm not so sure that's the problem. Look at the next page. In the last three months we've actually accepted three shipments that were originally identified as noncompliant."

"Meaning what?" Harry asked.

"I think the initial inspections were wrong."

"Wrong? What in the hell are they *doing* down there? Sounds like a training issue to me."

"That may be part of the problem," Joe replied. "The bigger issue, I believe, is the volume of components coming through the department. We're pushing out new products too fast. I think we're overwhelming the staff down there, particularly when you add all the rework and final inspections."

"I assume you've discussed this with Nancy?"

"I have."

"And...?"

"We either add more resources in that area or slow down our product development efforts."

"Can't happen," Harry answered abruptly. "Can't we move resources from another area?"

"I've considered that, but then we'd be short staffed somewhere else in the operation," Joe answered.

"Look, I don't mean to be a hard-ass about this, Joe, but our backs are against the wall here. We can't slow down the development cycle. Find a way to do more with what we have. Work it out with Nancy and get back to me in a couple of days." He gave the report back to Joe. "What else have you found?"

"Our customer support complaints have increased. That's created some friction between Customer Service and R&D."

"Who's running that operation down there?"

"Arnold Boyd."

"What seems to be the problem?" Harry asked.

"He wants more involvement in the development process." He avoided mentioning Arnold's dissatisfaction with the company's management.

"The kid's got a valid concern. I've known Kurt a long time and he can be a little protective of his domain sometimes. You'll have to nurture that relationship a little. Customer complaints travel quickly in this business."

"Harry, Mike Dunleavy is on line one. He says it's important." "Thanks, Alice," said Harry, acknowledging his assistant's interruption. "I'm sorry, Joe, but I need to take this call. Let's talk again soon. I'll be in New York until Thursday. See Alice about scheduling a meeting for sometime Friday."

As he returned to his office, he began to realize that this would not be as simple as he had expected. The issues facing AMD in general and Operations in particular were more complex than he had previously thought. Managing personalities and dealing with the resource issues had introduced new variables into his plan, which would force a change in his strategy. Nevertheless, he welcomed the challenge.

WHAT LUCY TAUGHT US

Cathy

Even at seven o'clock, the interstate was still sluggish. Thanks to Bob, however, Joe had discovered an alternate route to get home that avoided most of the evening traffic. In any case, it was still a thirty-minute drive to the one-bedroom apartment they had leased just outside of the city. Located above a retail store, it reminded him of their first apartment as newlyweds thirty years ago. It was certainly different from the house they had left behind, a four-bedroom in a cul-de-sac. As he arrived, he thought about the tremendous risk he had taken and what that had meant to his family. He sat in the car for a few minutes after turning off the engine wondering whether he had made the right decision.

Cathy met him at the door with a big hug. It was their daily ritual. "You look tired," she whispered. "I hope you're in the mood for Chinese tonight."

He smiled and hung his coat in the closet. Exhausted, he took a seat in the small L-shaped living room that doubled as his makeshift office. He loosened his tie and took off his shoes as she poured two glasses of their favorite Merlot. She could tell he was not in a good mood.

"So, how was your meeting with Harry?" she asked, sitting next to him on the couch.

"Like talking to the wall," he said sarcastically. He explained that Harry had brushed over his ideas and refused to address the staffing issue.

She listened silently as he went on to explain his concerns about customer service, the personality conflicts within his group, and the costly mistakes in Testing. On top of that, he was still trying to sort through the office politics and was not sure whom he could trust. She could hear the frustration in his voice.

The problems at AMD were a lot deeper than he had originally thought. He was confident he could fix the problems, but it would take time. Harry, it seemed, didn't understand that. The board was on his back to cut costs and to push more product out the door as quickly as possible. A prescription that simply creates more problems, Joe thought.

"Did you really think it would be that easy?" she asked.

"I anticipated some problems of course, but I'm not going to compromise my integrity by doing something I believe is wrong. If Harry has a problem with that, then maybe he should find another person to run the operation. I thought I had full authority to make changes, but it seems that's no longer the case." He paused for a moment to contain his anger. "Maybe I should have stayed at Star."

Cathy was not surprised. After thirty years, she knew Joe better than he knew himself. "I know you're frustrated, but you were bored at Star, and there's nothing you hate more than a routine job. I remember your first month there. You were just as unhappy, but eventually you found a way to get things done. You're a problem solver. It's what excites you. You just need to give it a little more time. Besides, you thrive on challenges."

She was right. During his ten years at Star, he had moved through the organization quickly, gaining a reputation as someone who could get things done. He had fine-tuned this skill without the type of authority he now had at AMD by enlisting the support of others. If he could possibly get a few of the other vice presidents on board, maybe Harry would listen and reconsider his opposition to his suggestions. It was a long shot, but the idea had potential.

Joe's brain was starting to rev up again when Cathy reminded him that dinner was getting cold. He was starving.

She showed him pictures of homes she had visited that day with Delores as they ate Chinese at the small folding table in the middle of the kitchen. They had both agreed to find a smaller home since they were now "empty nesters." Their daughter Sarah had graduated from college a year ago and had taken a job in Seattle. They missed her tremendously and anxiously hoped to see her during the holidays. With any luck, they would be in their new home by then.

After dinner, Cathy retreated to the bedroom to catch up on her reading while Joe stayed behind to review the current week's production reports. It had been a long day and he was tired. Before starting, he paused for a moment to reflect upon the support Cathy had given him in this move, and how blessed he was to have such a wonderful wife and friend.

Bob

After circling the block a third time, Joe finally spotted someone leaving a parking space on the opposite side of the street. He quickly made a U-turn in the middle of the street to lay claim to the space before someone else could. Fortunately, it was just a few blocks down the street from the diner where he had arranged to meet Bob Garcia.

Locals considered the Acme Diner an institution, and it was a big tourist attraction. The family-owned business had passed from generation to generation. A small, rather cramped place, its walls were adorned with pictures and autographs of celebrities who had eaten there over the years. As he entered the diner, he began looking for Bob, who he assumed would already be there. Sure enough, he spotted Bob in the rear of the diner waving to catch his attention. He made his way through the crowd to the back, where he greeted Bob with a hug.

"I thought I'd never find a parking space."

"Welcome to the big city," Bob said with a laugh while signaling for the server to come over. He moved his coat to another chair to make room for Joe.

"So how's the transition to city life going?"

"I like it, but it may take awhile for Cathy to get used to it. I do appreciate all the time Delores has spent with her. It's made the adjustment a lot easier."

"And the house search?"

"I haven't had much time to get involved with that. That's Cathy's domain. We're still waiting for an offer on our current house. It's a buyer's market. What can you do?"

The server handed each a menu and informed them of the specials for the day before leaving to seat customers that were still coming in the door.

"You're still at Lane College, right?

"In May it'll be six years. About a year ago I moved over to administration as an associate vice president for Enrollment Management."

"So, no more teaching?"

"That's right. I miss being in the classroom, but the opportunity was too hard to pass up. It's a great job, but it *does* have its moments."

The server returned to take their orders. She seemed somewhat impatient as they looked over the menu.

"Just coffee for me, please."

"I'll take the same," added Bob. "Decaf, black. Thanks. So what's going on over at AMD?"

"Sales are down for the third straight quarter, the competition is killing us, and our customer complaints seem to be growing each week. I've got internal turf battles going on, personnel conflicts, attendance issues..." he shook his head. "It's been a very interesting first month."

Bob joked, "Sounds like you're having fun!"

"Don't get me wrong. I'm not one to back down from a challenge. They hired me to fix those problems, and I intend to. The lack of teamwork between departments is what really concerns me. On top of it all, I can't seem to convince my CEO that we have a serious resource issue. 'Do more with less' is all I hear. He's completely focused on the bottom line at the expense of quality."

"That's interesting. We had a similar situation at the college about a year ago," said Bob.

"Believe me, Bob, nothing could be similar to this."

"No. Really. You'd be surprised," he replied. "My mandate, when I took this job, was to evaluate and recommend a better way to recruit and admit students. For us, it's a cradle-to-grave approach. We identify prospective students, nurture them through the admissions process, select the right candidates, and award financial aid if needed. Once they become students, we provide support services to get them through graduation. That's a major effort that involves many different departments and functions. At the end of the day, the success of this whole process depends entirely on our ability to work together as a team."

"OK. Make the connection for me," Joe said lightheartedly.

"If we drop the ball anywhere along that process, it affects the end result. We lose the student, or in your case, the customer."

"So how did you address issues across departments?" asked Joe.

"By looking at the overall process as a group of individual processes linked together. I felt if we could examine how we were doing things *within* each department, we might stand a good chance of identifying disconnects that might affect the process as a whole."

"Makes sense. But it seems like it would be a really involved undertaking," said Joe.

"Well it is; but it's well worth the effort. There's a video I'd like you to take a look at. I think that'll explain everything."

"Not another one of those management empowerment gurus, I hope," said Joe. "No thanks. I've seen my share of those."

"I think you'll enjoy this one," Bob said with a grin. "I'll e-mail it to you when I get back to the office."

They spent the next hour catching up on each other's lives and reliving old stories of their college days. It was hard to believe thirty years had passed so quickly. Eventually they realized it was time to get back to work.

"I've got a pretty tight schedule this afternoon, but let's do this again real soon. As a matter of fact, how about coming over to AMD? I'd love to give you a tour of the place."

"Sure. I'd like that," Bob said, reaching for the check.

"Good. I'll set that up and get back to you with a date. Thanks for the coffee."

By the time they both left the diner, the rain had stopped and the sun had started to peek through the clouds. As he got back to his car, he could see the bright orange fluorescent parking ticket under his windshield wiper. Time had obviously passed much quicker than he imagined.

Kurt

By the time he got back to the office, there were eight voice mail messages on his computer. The last two were marked URGENT. They were both from Kurt. Being able to listen to his voice mail through his computer still seemed rather incredible to him. He was amazed at how competent he had become using the system in just a few short weeks.

> *"Hello, Joe. This is Kurt. I need to see you as soon as you get in. It's very important. Please call me at extension 4710."*

Rather than call, he decided to take a walk down to see Kurt. It was always better to deal with urgent issues face-to-face. Kurt was in the middle of a design meeting with several engineers when Joe entered the R&D lab. In accordance with proper procedure, he put on the required safety equipment before entering the lab area. He was familiar with the routine now after having spent time in the department just a few days ago.

"Gentlemen, this might be a good place to take a break. Let's continue in about ten minutes," Kurt said, calling for a short pause in the session in order to speak with Joe. After dispersing the group, he led Joe back to his office.

"I've got a big problem with Nancy," he said, moving a stack of magazines from a chair for Joe to sit down. He closed the door to his office. After sitting down at his desk, he handed Joe an Exception Report.

"We received this from Testing this morning."

To Joe, it appeared to be a routine Exception Report for a component manufactured by one of their vendors.

"So what's unique about this?"

"Nancy's asked us to accept these components. The vendor has convinced her that the defect is negligible on the overall assembly."

"So what's your opinion?"

"It's a borderline condition. I recommend we send it back," he answered.

"What's the nature of the part and how do we use it?"

"They're lead fasteners that hold the shielding material in place inside the new Zoetrope X-ray machines. The samples tested are undersized, which is OK because they're within the tolerance range called out in the spec," Kurt explained.

"Then what's the issue?" asked Joe, appearing somewhat confused.

"The specification is wrong."

"What do you mean, 'wrong'?"

"The design requirements we sent over to Engineering were recorded incorrectly on the drawings that were, in turn, sent to the vendor. I checked the original design requirements against the final drawings this morning."

"So where does it fall within the correct range?" Joe asked.

"It's at the low end, and that's risky considering the use," Kurt responded.

Joe paused for a moment to collect his thoughts. He was starting to get a major headache. "Don't you see the specs and final drawings before they go out to the vendor?"

"We send the requirements to Engineering and they take it from there. We've always done it that way."

"So what happens now?"

Kurt removed his glasses and reclined back in this chair. He exhaled before speaking. "According to Nancy, it would take three weeks to get replacements from the vendor. That delays the actual production assembly and shipment to the customer by a month." Considering their current financial situation, Joe knew this wouldn't fly with Harry and the rest of the management team. Still, he knew he'd have to break the bad news to them eventually.

"Reject the Exception Report and have Nancy get the replacements moving ASAP. If she has a problem with that, have her see me," said Joe reluctantly. In the meantime, I'd like to see you, the Engineering manager, and Nancy in my office in an hour. I want to make sure these kinds of things don't happen again."

As Joe left the R&D area he couldn't help but wonder how many similar problems existed in the field that, unfortunately, were not being caught by accident.

Dinner

While waiting for his team to assemble, he paced around his office outlining in his mind how he would approach the problem. This was his first real test at AMD, and his team would be looking to him for leadership in light of the crisis. It could be a long night. To compound matters, it was Cathy's birthday. They had made dinner plans with Bob and Delores for later that evening. She had been looking forward to this day for quite some time. Hopefully, the reservation could be changed to a later time.

No one from his team had arrived yet, so he took the opportunity to call Cathy. He gazed through his window at the radiant collage of red, green, and yellow foliage while waiting for her to answer. It was a typical New England day for October.

"Hi, hon. I may be a little late for dinner tonight. I need to take care of an issue here. Maybe we should move our reservation back an hour or so."

"How long do you think you'll be?" she asked. He could tell from her voice that she wasn't too thrilled about the idea.

"Not sure. I'm hoping it won't take too long. Let's shoot for 7:30 instead. Remember to call Bob and Delores. Maybe I can meet you at the restaurant to save time."

"Don't forget it's a Friday night. What happens if that time's not available?"

Joe paused before answering. "Then I'll cut the meeting short and meet you there at 6:30," he said.

"Good answer. See you soon."

Crisis Management

Tom Wong was the first to arrive at Joe's office for the hastily arranged meeting. Tom was another member of the original startup team at AMD, having worked his way up through the organization to his current position as manager of Engineering.

While waiting for the others to arrive, he explained to Joe how his team of engineers worked with R&D to prepare designs and specifications for parts produced by their vendors. That working relationship, however, had grown a bit strained lately, driven by management's push to shorten the product development cycle. As a result, errors like the one under discussion had become more common and had become a source of friction between Kurt and himself.

Kurt and Nancy entered together and took seats directly across from Tom. The seating arrangement seemed to set the stage for the probability of a battle. It was almost inevitable, given that the problem affected all three areas. The challenge would be to avoid finger pointing and keep the conversation focused on solutions.

Joe started the meeting by getting right to the issue. He asked the team why design specs went straight to the vendor with no final review from R&D. As he expected, Kurt was the first to respond.

"Perhaps it might help if I explain the history behind that arrangement. In our early years, R&D and Engineering were actually part of the same department, so it was easy to collaborate with everyone together. As the business grew, the functions were split and Engineering was moved into the old warehouse area." He explained how the split and physical separation eventually took their toll on the quality of communications between the two. Over time, the internal politics and personalities created even more autonomy. As Joe listened, it brought back memories of his conversation with Charlotte a few weeks ago and her description of AMD as a collection of independent operations.

"Considering the current situation, is there a reason why R&D can't make a final review of the specs before release to the vendor?" Joe asked.

"We can, but it just means more work for us. We really shouldn't have to do that," Kurt said.

Tom disagreed. "I think it's reasonable to assume that these kinds of things will happen, given the volume of designs we're being asked to handle. Having an extra review of the final specs makes sense to me."

"I agree with Tom," added Nancy. "Our inspection team is struggling to keep up with the volume of incoming parts. If we don't move more resources into those areas these problems will continue."

More resources. It's an argument Joe had heard before. He informed the group that he had already raised those concerns with Harry, who was strongly against any product slowdowns or staff additions. They would simply have to find another way around that situation. Right now, however, he needed to focus their attention on addressing the Exception Report. He asked Tom to explain how specifications were currently prepared.

"It's pretty simple. All new designs start in R&D. Kurt provides a rough sketch and a few design requirements, and we develop that into an actual design. We use several high-end computers to create an actual model of the part. If needed, we'll consult with R&D to modify the design if there's an issue with the vendor's ability to produce the part. Once we get an order confirmation from Purchasing, we ship the specs off to the vendor to be made."

"That's fairly accurate; however, we do have situations when that changes," added Kurt. "For example, there are occasions when we handle all the design details, particularly for things like prototypes for customers."

"So in that situation, you work directly with the vendor to produce the prototype?" Joe asked.

"Yes. There's no need to get Engineering involved," he answered.

"And that becomes a problem for us when the prototype is actually converted to a final design," Tom said angrily. "In some cases it may be difficult to produce on a larger scale. By not involving us at that stage, we essentially end up redesigning the part."

Kurt responded by questioning the technical capabilities of the engineers in Tom's department. As they continued to argue back and forth, it was becoming apparent to Joe that there was no clear consensus on how or why things were done a particular way. At this point, his inclination was to mandate the final review and accept the consequences.

"There are clearly concerns on both sides. However, I'm convinced that all specs should be reviewed before they go to the vendor. I understand what that will do in terms of increased workload for everyone. We just can't afford to have these things happen. I've instructed Kurt to reject the Exception Report. I'll address the schedule delay with Harry."

Although his body language expressed disappointment with the decision, Kurt remained silent. For Nancy, another schedule delay meant a complete overhaul of her production and shipping plans for the next six weeks. All the same, Joe felt it was the right decision.

On their way out, Joe reminded the group that monthly reports were due on Monday. He needed their input for the report that went to Harry and eventually to the board. He quickly gathered his files, shut down his computer, grabbed his coat, and locked his office door behind him. It was 6:20; he was in luck. There was still time to make the 6:30 dinner reservation.

Lucy

"Good morning, Joe. There's a Bob Garcia in the lobby who says he has a 9:30 appointment with you."

"Thanks, Lois. I'll be down in a minute." He hung up the phone, neatly arranged a pile of papers on his desk, and placed a stack of production reports in a file cabinet. It had taken awhile, but, after several failed attempts, they had finally found a mutual time to meet. He was particularly interested in any suggestions Bob could offer to help him though his current dilemma. He took the back stairway on the way out instead of waiting for the elevator. That way he could bypass the crowd returning from the morning break. Bob had just completed the sign in process when he arrived at the lobby.

"Bob, welcome to AMD. It's good to see you. How about a cup of coffee before we start?

"That sounds good to me. I could use something to jump-start my brain this morning," he joked.

As they headed off to the café, Joe pointed out different parts of the operation. It was Bob's first exposure to an actual industrial operation and he seemed quite fascinated by it all. After getting their coffee, they continued their tour of the facility before finally making their way to Joe's office.

"So what do you think of the operation so far?"

Bob took a seat adjacent to a bulletin board covered with graphs and project timelines. "You've explained it to me a million times before, but now, after actually seeing it in person, I've got a much better understanding of how it all fits together."

"It's a synchronized process," Joe said. "When it works, it's great. But, coordinating people and departments to work together is a challenge here. I spend a good deal of my time on 'people issues.' That's basically what I'm struggling with."

"In some cases, people are a big factor in the execution of the process, but not always," said Bob. The two of them had hotly debated this point many times before. "I know we'll never agree on that point, but I'm open to listening to what you have to say. By the way, did you get a chance to watch the video I e-mailed last week?"

"Not yet. I've been too busy."

"It's only about five or six minutes long. Believe me, I guarantee it'll answer a lot of your questions. We can take a look at it now if you'd like."

Joe searched through his e-mail as Bob moved closer to the computer. They huddled around his desk. After locating the message, he clicked the link for the video on YouTube. It was an old episode from the *I Love Lucy* show.

After about a minute, Joe paused the playback. He was somewhat puzzled by the content. "Are you sure this is the video you meant to send?"

"I use this clip in several of my business classes. It's a classic episode. It pokes fun at role reversal, but the underlying message actually deals with processes and how we react to situations in the workplace," Bob explained.

"It looks familiar. I may have seen this before. It's been awhile, but as I recall it's got something to do with a bet between Lucy and Ricky, right?" asked Joe.

"Right. Fred and Ricky stay at home and do the housework, and Lucy and Ethel go out and work for a day. It's the old walk-a-mile-in-my-shoes philosophy. You can't understand or appreciate what I do each day until you try it yourself."

He continued. "A candy company hires Lucy and Ethel to wrap individual chocolates on a moving conveyor belt. They receive instructions from their supervisor explaining how to wrap each piece of candy, and are told that if any candy gets by them unwrapped, they'll be fired."

"Now, pay close attention to this part," said Bob, grinning as he restarted the video.

As they start the process of wrapping candy from the conveyor belt, Lucy and Ethel brag at the ease of the task. Gradually the conveyor belt speed increases, and the two start to miss several pieces of candy. In fear of losing their jobs, they start to hide unwrapped candy in their clothes, hats, and ultimately in their mouths to keep pace with the conveyor speed. It's a hilarious scene, filmed completely live and spontaneous. Soon the supervisor returns and, after being satisfied with their work thus far (i.e., all candy appears to be wrapped), orders the conveyor belt to speed up even faster and leaves.

"I've seen it a million times and it always cracks me up," said Bob, laughing.

"All right, Professor Garcia, break it down for me. What's the message here?"

"Well, let's start by analyzing the situation. Lucy and Ethel had no idea who produced the candy or how it even got on the conveyor belt. Their job was simply to wrap the candy and place it back on the conveyor. They had no idea where it would go next or who would handle it once it left their work area."

"So they understood only their own part of the process, but not necessarily how it fit into the overall process," added Joe.

"Right. With no communication or feedback on either end of the process, they couldn't control or negotiate the incoming speed or the output. Likewise, the workers supplying the candy were aware of only their operation and oblivious to the effect of any changes in speed downstream. In fear of losing their jobs, Lucy and Ethel chose instead to hide their mistakes from their supervisor. This created a false impression of their abilities, prompting the supervisor to increase the speed even more. We can only assume that this then led to even more problems."

"So you're saying it's the process that's at fault here, not Lucy and Ethel?

"Correct. It's the inefficiency of the process that encourages employees to find workarounds or create situations that lead to disconnects, delays, and, ultimately, to mistakes," Bob explained.

"So it becomes a matter of refining the process so that these types of things don't happen. That makes sense, but it's easier said than done. How would someone approach that?" asked Joe.

"First, it needs to be clear in people's minds what the whole process entails, and not just their portion. They must have an understanding of the process as a whole. They need to know how delays or mistakes affect other parts of the process downstream."

"That's true. I've got a situation right now involving my R&D and Engineering departments that's causing a major ripple in our production schedule. It could have been avoided if certain procedural steps had been in place."

"Procedures do help," Bob said. "At a minimum, they provide a measure of consistency. However, it sounds to me like you've got a classic case of silo mentality. They're all operating independently with little to no communication. I'd suggest bringing them all together to make sure each player understands not only his or her own role, but the role of everyone involved in the overall process."

"Good idea. That would also help to validate my perception of the entire process." Joe jotted down a few notes on a yellow pad. "As a matter of fact, why don't you facilitate that effort? You seem to have a really good grasp of this stuff. I'd be more than happy to compensate you for your time."

Bob thanked Joe for the offer, but was reluctant to commit, considering his already full schedule at the college.

"Just think about for a few days, then get back to me and we'll kick it around some more." It was a great idea and Joe was sure he could convince Bob to do it.

They spent the next half hour discussing how such a session would work and what it would need to achieve. Bob suggested they both think about it more and schedule a time to get back together to plan it in more detail. It was almost noon and he needed to get back to the college.

As they walked back down to the lobby, Joe continued to think about the video. The idea of process driving performance had shed a whole new perspective on his problem. He was beginning to see its potential, particularly as it related to the issues in his department. The challenge, however, would be finding a way to make believers of his staff.

Process

The Tuesday morning staff meeting was a standing meeting Joe had established to get his top management team together once a week. It was a means to discuss issues and to convey information from his senior staff meetings with the CEO. By starting at 8:00 a.m., there would be fewer distractions and interruptions. Arnold and Nancy were always there on time, while Kurt was typically late. This morning however, he was the first to arrive.

With all present and accounted for, he was able to start on time. "Unless anyone has an urgent issue to discuss, I'd like to use this meeting to share with you some discussions I've had recently with a colleague of mine. As you know, I've spent the last three weeks visiting each of your departments in order to get a better understanding of each operation. It's been a valuable learning experience for a variety of reasons."

"So, what's your overall impression?" asked Nancy.

"It's complex. On one hand, I was pleased to find most staff knowledgeable and committed to doing a good job. On the other hand, what I found to be most frustrating were the inconsistencies in the way we get things done around here."

"Amen!" Arnold exclaimed. "I've been saying that from day one."

Nancy asked Joe to clarify that statement. Kurt interrupted before he could respond.

"What he means is departments constantly change requirements to fit their needs at any given moment in order to meet production."

"If you're referring to Testing, I take offense to that comment," said Nancy, voice rising. "You know that's a lie."

Joe quickly intervened. "Let's not jump to conclusions or point any fingers here. In all fairness, I've witnessed this in *every* area. There doesn't appear to be any type of procedural structure in place that defines how things are done."

"I would agree. But, before we can establish structure, we, ourselves, need to be clear about the way things are done," added Arnold. "If you ask ten different people how something is done, you'll get ten different answers."

"That's not true in my area," said Kurt.

"I'm sure you understand how work gets done in your area, Kurt, but I would suspect there are people in other departments that have only a vague idea of what goes on in R&D," Arnold said. "I myself would be the first to admit it."

It was an interesting observation, Joe thought. As Bob had astutely pointed out during his tour, AMD appeared to suffer from a silo mentality.

"People, our overall objective is to deliver a quality product on time to the customer," Joe said. "To that end, each of you has a major role in that process. So any delays or errors we make in our own areas affect the product from beginning to end. From what I've seen so far, I believe the process, or lack of process, is at fault here."

"But that assumption completely ignores the fact that people are responsible for errors and delays," added Nancy.

"I'm not totally dismissing that fact," Joe responded, "but you'll find that the process itself sometimes encourages those errors or delays. Being human beings, we find ways to cover up those errors or delays, which just ends up compounding the problem.

"We need to step back and take a good look at how we get the work done in every area. That means understanding how

everything we do links together and drives the overall process."
He was on a roll now. "Every technician, inspector, supervisor,
and manager has to be on the same page for this to work."

"We realize the importance of doing this, but how do we go
about making it happen in a company like this? That's *my* main
concern," said Arnold.

Joe informed the group of his recent meeting with Bob and
their plan to conduct a brainstorming session to address that.
The purpose of the session would be to have the group develop
a strategy and a plan to constructively evaluate their processes.
He was eager to hear their thoughts.

After a moment of awkward silence, Kurt was the first to
speak and, after offering a few words of apology to Nancy, he
said, "I believe there's value in that approach and it's long over-
due. It might help to look at our issues objectively."

"You're preaching to the choir. When do we get started?"
asked Arnold.

Joe could sense a feeling of support. All eyes were now on
Nancy. She, however, remained silent, seemingly unconvinced
of the approach.

"The exact details are still being worked out. I hope to have
a firm date soon. For obvious reasons, we should probably take
this session off-site. Let's adjourn for now, that is, unless anyone has a pressing issue to bring before this group?" All three
remained silent.

As the others left, Joe could hear the phone ring again,
buried somewhere beneath the piles of paper on his desk. This
time, however, he was able to find it *before* it stopped ringing.

The Retreat

The Wannaker Inn seemed like the perfect place to hold an off-site meeting. Originally an old turn–of-the-century glove factory, it had been developed into a hotel while retaining many of its original fixtures and details. The inn had won a host of architectural awards over the years, and consistently ranked among the top hotel and convention centers in the area.

The meeting room selected for the retreat had a large mahogany table in the center surrounded by eight executive-style chairs. A large window in the rear of the room provided a picturesque view of the hotel's courtyard. The original exposed beams across the ceiling provided a unique link to its past. A small contingent of hotel staff worked diligently to complete the morning breakfast setup when Joe and Bob arrived.

Bob unpacked his laptop, projector, and handouts as Joe changed the seating arrangement to accommodate the smaller group. Joe reminded the hotel staff of his request for flip charts set up at each end of the table and a screen for the projector. Other than that, everything appeared to be fine.

The group hadn't arrived yet, so he took the opportunity to brief Bob on each person in the group. Bob sat down at the conference table and took out his notepad.

"Kurt, Arnold, and Nancy make up the core of my management team in Operations. Both Kurt and Nancy have been with the company since its start. Arnold, on the other hand, is a recent hire right out of graduate school. Needless to say, their personalities and backgrounds contribute to a wide difference of opinion as to how things should be done." He went on to describe Kurt as the more structured and disciplined member of his operation, while Arnold took a more textbook approach to his job.

"What Arnold lacks in actual experience, he makes up for in enthusiasm and his desire for change. Reminds me a little of myself when I took my first job out of college. He'll be your biggest advocate. That leaves Nancy. I would say she falls somewhere in the middle. She's the quiet one in the bunch, somewhat resistant to change. I'm convinced that attitude probably has more to do with job security than what's right for her department. Not a day goes by without some sort of disagreement or conflict among these three. It's an interesting mix."

"It most certainly is," Bob thought, as he continued to scribble notes on his pad. Now that he understood the players, he needed to know more about Joe's intentions, specifically, what he hoped to achieve by the end of the day.

"First and foremost, Bob, they need to resist the temptation to criticize how we currently get things done. This isn't intended to be a gripe session. I'd like you to help focus their attention today on developing a structured approach that we can use to examine and improve our processes. I think it's important that they themselves develop this approach, rather than having it dictated to them. If we can leave today with that accomplished, then I would say we're on the right track."

Just as he was about to continue his expectations, Arnold and Kurt arrived, with Nancy close behind pulling a rolling brief case. A hotel staff person carrying flip charts and a screen followed them. Joe greeted the group as they entered, and they responded in unison.

"Come in and make yourselves comfortable. Make sure you take advantage of this great breakfast spread too." Because they were a little behind schedule, he took the opportunity to start the introductions while they selected from the assortment of coffees, teas, and pastries at the back of the room.

"Folks, I'd like you to meet Bob Garcia. He'll be your facilitator today. Bob and I go way back, having known each other in college. As a matter of fact, we were roommates our freshman year. Bob's currently the associate vice president for Enrollment Management over at Lane College. I've asked him to come in today to help us develop a plan and methodology to improve our business processes." He motioned for Bob to take the floor as the group, breakfast in hands, took their seats around the table.

Bob thanked the group for giving him the opportunity to be of assistance, and explained how this session came to fruition. He informed the group that the two of them had discussed and planned this session for several weeks, and felt they had an agenda today that he hoped would be interesting, enlightening, and helpful.

"Would it help if we introduced ourselves?" asked Arnold.

"Well, I would guess you're Arnold Boyd. If that's correct, then the gentleman to my right would be Kurt and the woman in front of me, Nancy."

"Looks like you've been well prepared," Arnold said with a laugh.

"I've done my homework," he replied with a sly smile. "Before we get started, however, I'll let Joe share with you what we hope you'll take away from this session today."

Joe directed the team's attention to the screen displaying his PowerPoint presentation. "If you recall a few months ago at our first meeting, I laid out my plans to get AMD's operations back on track. I talked about a new vision to guide our business strategy that would focus on quality, reducing our development cycles and strengthening customer support. Having now seen your operations firsthand, however, it's clear to me that our immediate challenge is not connected to strategy. I've expressed my concerns on several occasions with this group about the way we get the work done. That concern involves not only the processes in your individual departments, but also those processes that move work among your departments." He waited a moment for a response. After a moment of silence, he continued.

"We need to take an objective look at our current processes and determine a way to make them operate more efficiently. The question, however, is how? What methodology do we embrace? And how do we sustain that?"

"Equally important, I feel, is the need to institutionalize this methodology across the operation," added Arnold. "Any improvements in our processes simply create a bottleneck elsewhere in the operation."

"Arnold makes a good point," Bob interjected. "The research would support that conclusion. Consider yourselves *pioneers*, if you will, of a new management philosophy within the organization. Your success can decide the future of the organization."

"That's correct," said Joe. "Focusing on process is a complete paradigm shift for AMD. It's necessary, and it's unavoidable if we hope to restore this organization to its full potential. Your goal today is to create that methodology." With that directive, he made his exit, leaving Bob and the rest of the team to conceptualize and finalize a solution.

Brainstorming

The team was somewhat surprised and disappointed that Joe would not be participating in the retreat. Bob explained to them that it was his decision not to involve Joe. In Bob's experience, not having management staff present created a more open and less threatening setting for discussion.

"Hopefully, by now, you've all had an opportunity to watch the *Lucy* video that I forwarded to Joe—correct?" They all nodded in agreement. "That's a good place to start our discussion." Before he began, he acknowledged Nancy's raised hand.

"I've heard that these types of evaluations always end with people losing jobs. Is that the intention here?"

"That's a good question, Nancy. The answer is no, that's not the intention of this effort. It is possible, however, that in the final analysis, jobs may be eliminated or combined with others, but that's usually balanced by moving staff to other areas that are understaffed. Does that answer your question?" Her nod implied yes.

"Now, let me raise a question. If I asked you to produce a diagram that describes how work is accomplished in your areas, what would that diagram look like?"

Arnold was the first to speak. "Probably...an organizational chart? It would show the structure and the relationships among the various departments."

"I would say a flowchart," said Kurt, "that shows the step-by-step flow of activities within the department. Taken one step further, it could also show the flow of activities among departments as well," he added, peering over his glasses at Bob.

"And you, Nancy?" Bob asked.

"I would agree with Arnold, particularly if we're concerned about the overall process across the organization."

"To a certain extent, you're all partially right. An org chart identifies the organization's reporting structure. While that's important to know, it doesn't describe *how things get done* in the organization. On the other hand, Kurt's idea of a flowchart gets us closer to our goal, but fails to identify who or what department is involved in each step of the process."

Bob turned toward the screen and advanced the PowerPoint presentation to a slide that appeared, at first glance, to be a flowchart. Upon scrutiny, however, it appeared to have decidedly different characteristics.

"This type of diagram is typically referred to in the industry as a *business process* map." He used his pointer to highlight several items on the slide. "As you can see, it's laid out in such a way as to clearly describe each step in a process, along with identifying the person or department responsible for carrying out these steps. A diagram like this makes it very clear in everyone's view how a particular process is performed. It also helps to establish consistency for those things that need to be repeated the same way, time after time."

"That's a rather complex-looking diagram. Are you asking us to develop something like that for all our processes?" asked Nancy.

"It's a good place to begin. However, the level of detail is entirely up to you. As a start, just a simple high-level diagram of your end-to-end process would probably be sufficient. Beyond that, you can always drill down deeper into each step, if needed. The most difficult part of this exercise is not the diagram itself, but making sure the description accurately reflects the process. In a lot of cases you'll find a variety of different perceptions regarding how things are done."

"Wouldn't the individuals actually involved in the process be the best source to engage in this effort?" asked Kurt.

"That would certainly seem to be the case. However, sometimes there are discrepancies even among that group. It's always a good idea to get as many stakeholders as possible involved in this step. The goal, at this point, is to arrive at what we call an *as-is* diagram. Once that's documented, the next step is to analyze the diagram to identify the problem areas." Between the nods, raised eyebrows, and note taking, he could sense they were starting to open up to the concept.

"Let's back up a minute and talk about why this is so important. First, some goal or objective must drive the whole notion of process improvement. Otherwise, what's the point? The objective should involve reducing, eliminating, or improving some function or characteristic of the process that's currently unacceptable."

"Like reducing the amount of time to assemble and test a final product," said Kurt, looking directly at Nancy as he spoke.

"Or reducing the amount of paperwork associated with a product return," added Arnold.

"And how do we accomplish that?" Bob asked.

"By analyzing the processes that drive those conditions?" said Nancy, somewhat uncertain in her answer.

"Absolutely," exclaimed Bob. "It's a simple concept, but for some reason, we tend to get bogged down in focusing on the people involved instead of the processes."

As the discussion went on through the morning, he could tell from their body language that they were starting to suffer from information overload. Rather than continue, he decided it would be a good time for a break. That would give him an opportunity to prepare for the major activity later that morning.

Exercise

After a few coffee refills and several phone calls back to the office, they appeared refreshed and ready to get started on their working session. Bob asked that they work as a group for the next hour or so. Their assignment would be to come up with an objective, select the related process, determine how it would be documented and who would be involved in this effort, and, finally, create a strategy to analyze the process.

Huddled at one end of the table with a flip chart, the three began their discussions. At this point, the conversational tone appeared cordial. As they began their deliberation, Bob opened a note that a hotel staff person had left during the break. It was a message from Joe to call at his first opportunity.

To avoid disturbing the group, he ventured out into the hotel courtyard to make the call.

"Hi, Joe. Just returning your call."

"So, how are things going?"

"Great. Things are moving right along. They're in the middle of the strategy session right now."

"Any issues at this point?

"No. They seem to be a very sharp bunch. I think we'll end up with some very interesting results."

"If I can get out of the office this afternoon, I'll stop by at the end of the session. If not, we can debrief over dinner tonight," said Joe.

"That's fine. Give me a call later and we'll work something out."

Rather than return to the conference room, he decided to stay out in the courtyard for a while longer. After all, it was probably one of his last opportunities to enjoy a beautiful fall afternoon before the impending Northeast winter.

Lunch

The group had worked diligently through the morning. Rather than interrupt their momentum, Bob allowed the session to continue until lunchtime. After lunch, if they needed more time, he could readjust the afternoon agenda.

The hotel's staff arrived at 11:45 to begin setting up for lunch, which he felt was probably a good point to break for the morning. He was curious to know how things were going so far.

"I think it's going well at this point. This has been an eye-opening session for me," said Arnold. "In some cases it confirms what I assumed went on in Nancy's and Kurt's areas. I was also surprised to learn a few things that I wasn't aware of."

Bob was excited about the potential of this group and looking forward to their final ideas and suggestions this afternoon. For now, however, he was ready to eat. The hotel had provided an exceptional lunch selection with an assortment of hot and cold dishes. They adjourned for the morning and made their way to the table at the back of the room.

"So how did you get involved in this process stuff?" Kurt asked as he picked from the assortment of cold cuts on one of the platters.

"When I moved into my current position at Lane, my directive was to improve our end-to-end process for recruiting and, subsequently, graduating students. Similar to your situation, that involves many different offices that must work together. I discovered that many of our problems involved the handoffs between departments. Like most people, I assumed it was a *people* issue. After doing a little research, however, I came across a series of articles related to process improvement. One article in particular discussed how foreign competition in the late '70s forced American businesses to closely examine how they were doing business. At that time, the industry's solution was to employ efficiency experts to examine their processes."

"Oh, I distinctly remember that," said Nancy. My husband lost his job because of those so-called experts. I'll never forget the strain that caused for us."

"That definitely created a bad image throughout the industry. While reducing staff did streamline processes and produced some added value, up to a point, continued staff reductions failed to yield any additional value."

"The law of diminishing returns," added Kurt, his mouth full of food.

"Exactly. So there had to be some other controlling mechanism going on. That's what led me to turn my attention to the process, as opposed to the people involved in the process. One evening while watching TV at home, I happened to stumble across the *Lucy* episode on one of those late night cable channels. From that point on, it was clear."

"So the sixty-four-thousand-dollar question is: how does one constructively evaluate a process?" said Arnold.

"Constructively? Yes, that is, indeed, the challenge, along with *sustaining* any changes made to that process," added Bob.

After a brief silence, Kurt asked, "Have the desserts arrived yet?"

The Presentation

After lunch, the group continued to work quietly on their assignment with only an occasional flare-up, only to return to normal minutes later. On several occasions, they stopped to ask Bob to clarify certain points or to seek his advice.

Just prior to the afternoon break, they notified Bob that they were ready to discuss their ideas. In an unexpected move, Nancy assumed the spokesperson's role and proceeded to go through the points outlined on the flip chart.

"After much debate," she said, looking at Kurt, "we decided to address the need to reduce the amount of time it takes to inspect incoming parts from our vendors."

"What's the current situation?" asked Bob.

"Vendors produce parts for us that we, in turn, use to assemble the final product for our customers. They're given a specification from our Engineering group that guides the manufacture of that part. We test several samples for compliance to our spec after receiving the finished parts. Any samples that fail to meet the spec go to Kurt's group in the form of an Exception Report. They make the decision to accept the shipment or reject it."

"OK. Now narrow that down to the specific problem," said Bob.

"We operate on pretty tight delivery schedules, particularly with our larger customers. Obviously, if we reject any noncompliant parts, the time required to rework or receive replacements impacts that schedule. We've lost customers as a result."

"So the primary objective would be what?"

"The primary objective of our analysis would be to streamline this process in order to minimize the impact of a schedule change," said Arnold.

"I assume you have data to use as a benchmark to quantify what you would consider as an acceptable improvement, correct?" asked Bob.

"We do," Nancy answered.

"So the objective is clear. Good. What's next?"

"The next step would be to get consensus on how the current process is managed and performed. That would ensure that everyone involved—specifically Shipping and Receiving, Testing, and R&D—understands and agrees how this process is currently done. Essentially, who does what and how."

"It would also enforce everyone's understanding of how mistakes or delays on their part affect the overall timeline," added Kurt.

"OK. So what's your strategy to get everyone to agree on what that current process looks like?" asked Bob.

"We discussed that at length and decided it would be best to interview each individual involved in the process," said Nancy. "That way, we could gain a better understanding of specific roles. Each of us has a general idea of how we think the process rolls out, but I'm sure we'd be surprised to find out from the users how things are really done."

"The interviews would then allow us to construct a picture of the process, or, as you say, an as-is diagram," added Arnold.

"I'd recommend vetting that diagram with the individuals interviewed to confirm its accuracy," Bob suggested. So far, he was impressed with their plan. "So, what happens next?"

Nancy turned to the outline on the next page. "We agreed that this process diagram should be evaluated by a group of stakeholders. Their goal would be to question the way the process currently works. Also, to focus on ways to streamline, eliminate, or combine tasks where possible. We also recommend attaching time limits and procedures to specific tasks."

"Can you give me an example?"

She glanced at Kurt before speaking. "Well, when we submit an Exception Report to R&D for a decision, it shouldn't take any more than two days for an answer. Right now, there's no standard window for a response." All heads turned toward Kurt.

"I'm not sure that's possible to quantify, Nancy. Some requests require more analysis than others. Remember, we're a small group. We simply can't drop whatever we're doing each time we receive an Exception Report."

"I agree," said Bob. "In some cases it is difficult to gauge how much time a particular task should take to complete. In those situations, setting a reasonable range of expectation would be sufficient."

Arnold approached the flip chart to explain the next several points. "The next step would be to select a team to evaluate the process diagram. It was obvious to us that it should involve staff engaged in the actual process. They're the best source for ideas or suggestions to improve what they do on a daily basis. We also decided to include a few individuals outside of the process as well. We wanted a balanced, unbiased analysis of the process."

"So, essentially, the process would be evaluated by a cross-functional team. That's an interesting idea," said Bob.

"Now we've got a question for you," said Arnold. "What happens if someone on the evaluation team is threatened by a suggestion to change or eliminate a task or job they currently perform? Their conscious or subconscious resistance might disrupt the team's efforts. We weren't able to agree on a way to address that."

It was an excellent question. He thought about it for a second before answering. "That's certainly a very real possibility if you include actual job performers. I would suggest taking time at the beginning of the effort to train the team so they're aware of this potential roadblock. I've used an excellent book as a training guide in similar situations at the college. It's *The Five Dysfunctions of a Team* by Patrick Lencioni. It discusses common team concerns such as the absence of trust, fear of conflict, lack of commitment, accountability, and so on. The team should be aware of these roadblocks before they start their review."

Bob went on to explain how they could also help the evaluation team to work through these types of issues by being available to facilitate the review sessions. Clearly, a future session with Kurt, Arnold, and Nancy could address this matter in more detail. "Right now, I believe you're on track. It appears to be a solid strategy. Good work." He was sure Joe would be enthusiastic.

"So how do we convince management to follow through with the evaluation teams' recommendations?" Nancy asked.

"Getting management buy-in can be tough. Fortunately, Joe's a VP, so he has the authority to implement the team's recommendations. That shouldn't be a problem. What you will encounter, however, will be resistance by those who'll be affected by the change. It's a natural reaction."

That struck a chord with Arnold. Change was his personal mantra. AMD staffers had perceived him as a rebel in the company from day one, and he had continuously encountered opposition to his ideas. He had real concerns about this part of the effort.

Arnold was visibly upset. "How can you expect to change a group of people who for so long have been conditioned to do things a certain way? That mentality starts at the top and filters down the organization."

"I agree; it's tough. It's probably the hardest part of the whole effort," Bob explained. "That's partially our fault. We make the critical mistake of trying to force change upon people. Very little effort is ever made to build the case for change."

He assured the group that there were strategies to address that aspect as well and suggested they meet for another session later to discuss change management. For now, he felt they were off to an excellent start and suggested they review their plan with Joe as a next step. He agreed to be available to the group to offer advice or to answer any questions as they advanced through the process.

"We'd like to thank you for taking the time to lead us through this effort. Speaking for the group, I'd say it's been a very productive day," said Arnold.

"It's been my pleasure. I'm sure I've learned just as much from you today as you have from me. I've enjoyed the experience as well," said Bob.

As they began preparing to leave, he took the opportunity to call Joe to confirm their plans to meet later that evening. After a few unsuccessful attempts, he left a voice message followed by a quick e-mail to Joe. Kurt was still lingering over the dessert tray in the back of the room.

"It's OK if you want to take those with you, Kurt."

"Are you sure?"

"Yeah, I'm sure. Help yourself," he said with a chuckle.

Debriefing

After receiving a call from Joe, they agreed it would be easier to meet at the Inn. That would give Bob time to collect his notes and to summarize a few observations for his meeting with Joe. He suggested they meet at the bar, adjacent to the front lobby.

Bob was finishing his second cup of coffee by the time Joe arrived. He was in the process of organizing his notes for a final report he had committed to provide at the end of the session.

Eventually, Joe made his way over through the standing room only happy hour crowd. As he sat down, he motioned to a nearby server to place his order.

"Double martini, with a twist of lemon."

"Sounds like you had a *good* day."

"Unbelievable," Joe answered. "Just as you think you're finally making progress, everything falls apart again. Some people just don't get it."

"Been there," said Bob.

"In spite of it all, there *is* some good news today. Our offer on the house in Sand Lake was accepted this morning."

"That's great! I'm sure Cathy must be excited."

"She loves the house and the neighborhood. Now we can finally move out of that apartment and get back to a more normal life. Please thank Delores for all the work she's done. She really deserved the sale. Now if we can only sell our existing house." He took a sip of the martini the server had just left.

"So, how did the rest of the day go for you and the team?"

"It was productive. Despite their differences, they're a good group. I think they understand the concepts. It'll be interesting to see them put it into action."

"What's the plan?"

"They plan to look at the incoming inspection process."

"Good place to start! We're dealing with several issues in that area right now. There's a riff between R&D and Testing."

"I could feel the tension between Nancy and Kurt on several occasions. What's the problem?"

"Errors were made on a spec sent to a vendor. The parts were produced in accordance with the error on the spec. Kurt wants to reject the shipment, causing Nancy to miss her shipment date by at least three weeks. Normally, we can negotiate with the customer for slipping a date, but this happens to be a customer who's threatening to buy from our competition."

"It definitely sounds like a process issue to me," said Bob.

"I agree. I can't wait for them to get started."

"I'll send you a summary of what was discussed, along with my observations. There are, however, some things you'll need to do."

"Such as?" asked Joe, as he took another sip of his martini.

"For starters, take an honest and objective look at their final recommendations. I know you're committed to this, so that shouldn't be a problem. They'll need to feel that their work is valued and appreciated. Provide a gift or some sort of company award as recognition. That's important. Next, start a media blitz to prepare the affected areas and staff for change. In order to get people to buy in to the recommended changes, they'll need to understand why this change is happening. Make the connection between the need for change and company sales, profits, or goals. Finally, you'll need to find a way to entrench process improvement into the culture of the organization. Once you start, you can't stop. It's an ongoing process."

"That all makes sense, I suppose. My concern is sustaining the improvements. How can we be sure a year from now that people won't slip back into their previous routines?

"That's a valid concern. Unfortunately, I don't have an answer for that. We'll see what the team recommends," said Bob, checking his watch.

"I do need to leave soon," Joe said, taking one last sip of his drink. "Cathy and I are going out tonight to celebrate. I really appreciate the work you've done. Let's get together again in a week or two, after I've met with the team."

"Sure. I'd love to see how it all unfolds. I did mention to them that I'd be available if needed," added Bob.

"That's great. Well, I'm outta here. Say hello to Delores for me."

As he turned to leave, he remembered one final item he needed to discuss with Bob.

"Oh, and your check is in the mail," he said with a laugh.

Harry Revisited

The board meeting had been delayed for several hours due to weather conditions that had caused travel problems for various members. As a result, Joe was able to spend more time preparing his report for Harry. He had asked Joe for an update on the cost-cutting initiative so he could brief the board, and had scheduled a short session with Joe to go over the report.

"Hello, Joe? This is Alice. Harry needs to get over to the Wannaker Inn early to meet with a few board members before the meeting. He'd like to review your report on the way over to the meeting. Can you meet him downstairs in ten minutes?"

"Yeah, sure." He hung up and quickly gathered the documents, which were scattered all over his desk. On his way out, he made a quick call to Cathy. Today was moving day. The moving company was scheduled to arrive before noon to begin packing. Joe hoped he could get home before they arrived.

As he reached the lobby, he could see the company van parked out front. Harry was waiting inside, on his phone as usual.

"Hello, Joe. So, what do you have for me?"

"Here's a copy of the initiatives and where we stand," Joe replied.

"Just give me a brief summary. I'll read the memo later."

"There's not much room to work with our vendors on getting the cost of our parts down, but we do see an opportunity to minimize our returns. Also, if we tighten up the movement of our parts through assembly and shipping, we can negotiate delivery incentives from our customers. The numbers on the report summarize our potential savings."

"OK. Good. What about that issue down in Nancy's area?"

"We're looking at ways to handle the volume. I've had a consultant work with the team to look at ways to streamline that process."

"Let me know how that goes," said Harry. "I'm meeting with a few of the board members in a half hour to discuss our operating costs. I suspect they'll push for a two or three percent reduction in staff at the full board meeting this afternoon."

"Across the company?" asked a startled Joe.

"I would imagine. Given the market conditions, it's unavoidable. If your strategy to streamline the testing process works, we may need to implement that across the company." The van pulled up in front of the hotel to let Harry out. "We'll talk later," he said, stuffing Joe's report in his briefcase as he got out of the car.

"Where to, sir?" asked the driver.

Joe failed to answer. He was deeply concerned about the impact a reduction in staff would have on his plans. Harry was right. It was probably unavoidable.

"I'm sorry. AMD, please," he answered.

Update

Thank God, it's Monday, Joe thought. The move last weekend had been painful. In addition to the move from their apartment to the new house, movers were also delivering their belongings from their old house. He had never seen so many boxes in one place. It was a challenge to find anything at this point.

Arnold entered the conference room and took a seat across from Nancy and Joe. He informed the group that Kurt had made a quick stop for coffee and would arrive in a few minutes. They began discussing the agenda as Kurt walked in.

"Coffee, anyone?" asked Kurt as he entered the conference room with coffee pot and cups.

"No thanks, Kurt," Joe responded. "Let's start with an update on your project with Bob; then, we can go over some of the details that came out of the board meeting this weekend."

Nancy passed out a diagram to each person. "So far, Kurt, Arnold, and I have interviewed every person involved with the inspection process. We've also talked to staff in R&D and the assembly areas. The diagram I've handed out is the result of those conversations. It's a little rough, but it's clear enough to give a basic understanding of what happens and who's responsible for doing what." She allowed Joe a few moments to look over the diagram before continuing.

"We've verified the diagram with the individuals interviewed. It took a few iterations to get consensus, but we're there." Nancy spent the next ten minutes going through the diagram, step by step, explaining each task. Joe was impressed. It appeared to be a very comprehensive effort.

"It was very enlightening to discover a lot of misunderstandings regarding the process, even among staff in the same department," said Arnold.

"That's interesting, but not at all unexpected," Kurt said.

"So, where are we now?" asked Joe.

"We've assembled a team to look at the diagram as it now stands," answered Nancy. "The majority of the group includes staff who are actually involved in the process, and a few others who are not directly involved at all. We thought it would be a good idea to get an outside point of view, so we added two people from the sales force to the mix. Their input should help the group understand the process from the client's perspective.

"Right now, the group is meeting several times a week to analyze the process. Their mandate is to look for opportunities to streamline the process by eliminating redundant or unnecessary tasks and to determine where documented procedures might be helpful. We expect to have their recommendations late next week."

"Excellent. If we were to extend this approach across the rest of the company, how would we roll it out?" Joe asked.

They were surprised to hear that, and not quite sure where he was going with that comment. They looked at each other and waited for someone to speak first.

"The approach is rather straightforward," said Arnold. "Select a process, form an evaluation team, and look for opportunities. There may be issues with that on a broader level, however."

"Such as?"

Arnold explained that they were able to justify to their staff why improving the process was so important. They were very careful to avoid any mention of people losing their jobs because of the study.

Expanding this across the organization would make it harder to address those fears, he added. Unless it came explicitly from top management, the rumor mill would work against the effort.

Joe got up and closed the conference room door for privacy. After sitting back down, he informed them that what he was about to tell them was highly confidential. "There's been no official decision yet, but the board is considering a three percent staff reduction across the organization. If that happens, we'll need to find ways to manage our operation with less staff. This process approach might help in that respect."

"I'm not at all surprised," fumed Nancy.

"Neither am I," added Arnold.

Kurt simply shook his head in disbelief, while nervously tapping his pen on the tabletop.

"I'm not ready to throw in the towel yet," Joe said. "I think there's still time to get through this slump. The South American project looks like a possibility, so let's keep our fingers crossed. In the meantime, we should begin preparing for this possibility.

"We need to start thinking about extending this process analysis approach to every process in our operation, and anticipate how it might roll out company wide." He suggested the three continue to meet to identify other processes in their areas that might benefit from this approach, particularly if fewer staff were to perform it.

"Let's get back together as soon as your evaluation team has completed their recommendations," Joe said.

As he headed back to his office, Joe made a mental note to call Bob to talk more about the process analysis concept. If he could prove its value in operations, then it might be possible to sell Harry on a company-wide implementation of the approach. Even if the staff reduction did not happen, it would still be extremely helpful in improving their existing processes throughout the company.

Recommendations

As Nancy had promised, the evaluation team completed its analysis of the inspection process, and submitted its recommendations the following Friday. Nancy, Kurt, and Arnold met the following Monday morning to review the findings. They were impressed with the team's efforts and found many of the suggestions thought provoking and insightful. After meeting with the evaluation team to clarify a few of the recommendations, they agreed to schedule time to meet with Joe. At Joe's request, they invited Bob Garcia to attend as well.

As they assembled in the conference room, Nancy began by passing out copies of the team's recommendations along with copies of the original process diagram and the revised diagram created by the evaluation team.

"As a group, we reviewed the suggestions and recommend pursuing those that are highlighted in red." She briefly summarized each one, discussing the potential value. Suggestions included testing for compliance *at the vendor's site* for large or time-sensitive shipments, processing Exception Reports *electronically* with workflow software and electronic signatures, requiring Engineering to submit specifications to R&D for review and final sign-off *before* sending them to vendors and, finally, cross training personnel in the assembly area to assist with incoming inspections as needed.

They all agreed that the recommendations had great potential. Joe questioned what would be required to implement the recommendations, and how soon that could happen.

"There are a few details that need to be worked out," added Arnold. "For example, we feel the on-site inspection will be a tremendous time-saver for us, but we'll need to negotiate with each vendor the cost of sending one of our inspectors to their site. It may be possible to add that as a contract requirement. Implementing a workflow system and electronic signatures for Exception Reports will require purchasing the necessary software. We've already asked the IT department to research products and get us a cost."

Kurt addressed the sign-off recommendation. "After we develop the specifications for a new product, we send it over to Engineering to develop the drawings and final specs used by the vendor to build the part. It goes from their office directly to the vendor. As you know, there's always an opportunity for an error in the translation of the documents between our office and Engineering. Sending it back to us for final sign-off should take care of that problem. We've resisted that in the past, but I'm willing to go along with the recommendation of the team. It's a matter of getting the two departments together to work out the details of the additional step."

"As far as cross training is concerned," said Nancy, "the team felt that we could manage the increasing amount of rework and incoming inspections by shifting staff from the Assembly area as needed. This strategy would also help us if we were forced to cut staff across the department."

"Fantastic! Those are all great recommendations." Joe was thrilled. "I'd like each of you to come up with a plan to implement the recommendations affecting your area. Specifically, I'd like you to define benchmarks and think of ways to measure the changes so we can gauge their level of success over time. Bob, is there anything you'd like to add?"

"I agree. Those *are* great recommendations. My only suggestion would be to make sure you work closely with HR to rewrite job descriptions for any staff affected by process changes. Also, be sure to reward the evaluation team for its efforts. They've done a tremendous job and that needs to be recognized within the organization."

Bob agreed to stay on after the meeting to work with Arnold, Kurt, and Nancy to discuss benchmarking and measurements. Joe, on the other hand, returned to his office to begin planning the next step in his strategy to continue the process analysis effort within his operation.

Progress

It had been a month since his management team had implemented most of the process improvement recommendations, and Joe was excited to finally see some of the preliminary data. The implementation had been relatively painless with only a few tweaks and modifications needed in the field. After acting on a recommendation by one of the inspectors, he had begun receiving a flood of suggestions from operations staff for other processes to examine for improvements.

As he pored over the data, he was curious to find all areas reporting significant improvements, with one exception—customer complaints. The number of component rejections had dropped because of on-site inspections, Exception Reports were being processed 10 percent faster, and the extra help in the assembly area appeared to be keeping up with the increased workload. Finally, specification reviews by R&D prior to their release to vendors had eliminated any errors in translation. He had hoped for these types of results. The number of customer complaints, however, remained relatively constant. Although they had not addressed that issue in the process exercise, he felt it might be a good candidate for the next iteration of the team's evaluation efforts. In his excitement, he decided to forward a copy of the data to Bob via e-mail so he too could see the results of his efforts working with the team.

The next step would be to encourage his managers to sustain this progress. If he could show consistency in the trends, he would then have a solid case to take to Harry.

Celebration

As a way of showing their appreciation for the work accomplished, Joe and his management group had arranged to take the evaluation team to dinner. They all planned to meet after work at the Wannaker Inn. Bob Garcia had planned to attend, but had a last-minute change of plans. Joe had also asked Harry to attend, but had not heard from Alice, his assistant, to determine if his schedule would permit such a visit.

The group gathered at the bar as they waited for the full party of ten to get there before being seated in the dining area. By the time Joe arrived, Nancy was already there. She pulled him aside to speak with him in private.

"Joe, I'd like you to know that I've really enjoyed working for you these last few months. When you started, we—that is, Kurt, Arnold, and I—weren't sure what to expect. Kurt and I have been onboard since the beginning and we share a deep desire to see AMD survive." She paused before continuing. "This 'process' stuff has opened up a whole new world for me. For the first time, I've been able to understand what happens outside of my area. I also think it's been helpful in getting Kurt and Arnold on the same page. I just wanted to personally express my appreciation for the job you're doing at AMD. We're glad you're here."

Joe was practically speechless. After the initial shock, he thanked her and acknowledged her work as being critical to the success of the effort thus far. Before he could continue, he realized that everyone in the group had arrived, and had started making their way toward the dining area. They proceeded to follow. Joe hoped he would have a chance to continue the conversation with Nancy during the evening.

The maitre d' and his staff had done a superb job of setting a very fancy table for ten. Kurt selected a couple of bottles of vintage wine for the group, as they all scanned their menus. Once everyone had ordered dinner and received a glass of wine, Joe interrupted the table chatter to offer a toast.

"I'd like to take a moment to congratulate this team for all of the fine work it's done. We certainly appreciate your efforts and your honesty in helping to move the company forward." With that, he raised his glass as they all joined in the toast.

"As a token of our gratitude, we have a little gift for each of you." Joe signaled for Kurt to begin handing out packages that he had placed under the table. He asked that they wait until the end of the evening to open the gifts.

People seemed to be enjoying themselves as the evening progressed. The food was outstanding, and the wine continued to flow. Joe was relieved to know that the hotel would be directly billing AMD for this outing. As he began to survey the group's interest in dessert, he was surprised to see a familiar figure approaching the table. The team was likewise stunned to see their CEO.

"Sorry I can't really stay. I'd love to join you, but I've got a million things to do this evening. I just wanted to stop by to give my personal thanks to each of you for a fine job. It's people like you who've made AMD what it is today."

Joe, still somewhat amazed, thanked Harry for his support of the team's efforts.

"I've had a chance to study the early results, Joe. I think it looks impressive. Call Alice in the morning to set up a time for us to talk. I want to move forward with this idea across the rest of the company."

As he turned to leave, Harry stopped to give the group another bit of good news. "Incidentally, looks like we'll all be pretty busy over the next two years. We just closed the South American deal."

With that, the group let out a collective roar and a succession of high fives, much to the displeasure of their fellow diners. It was truly a great ending to a great night.

Shirts

"Cathy, where did we put my shirts?" Joe had been opening box after box for the last ten minutes, looking for a shirt to wear. After a month in the new house, things were still disorganized. For the most part, they were still living out of boxes. She suggested he look downstairs in the basement, which had served as the main storage area for most of the boxes.

"That's the first place I looked. I can't find anything down there."

"Did you try the closet in the hallway?" He had forgotten about that.

"Found them. Thanks." He was in luck. There was only one clean shirt left in the box.

He dressed quickly and kissed Cathy good-bye as he left the house. Even though he was only a few minutes behind, he would have to take another route to work. He had finally mastered the trials and tribulations of driving in the Northeast. As he waited to get onto the interstate highway, he took a moment to reflect upon his decision to leave Star Manufacturing. In the course of a year, he had left a secure job with a future, and a great neighborhood and friends. In its place, he had joined an unstable company with a very specialized product line, inherited a rather dysfunctional staff, and encountered a daily barrage of customer complaints. On top of that, he was now making two monthly mortgage payments, which had significantly affected his retirement plans. Had he known what he was getting himself into, would he have made the move? He thought about it for a minute.

Yeah. He'd do it all over again. In a heartbeat.

The Model

Business processes drive the creation and delivery of every organization's products and services. More specifically, processes can be viewed as *the way things get done*. In theory, their design ensures consistency in delivery. More commonly, however, the individuals involved must interpret, define, and follow the processes. This sets the stage for inconsistencies, confusion, delays, and miscues.

Viewing an organization as a system rather than a vertical reporting relationship (i.e., an organizational chart), enables us to see how work actually gets done through processes that cut across functional boundaries. The greatest opportunity for performance improvement, therefore, lies at those points where a function or task becomes a "handoff" from one department or function to another. These critical interfaces that often occur in the "white spaces" of a traditional organizational chart become clearly visible in the process view of an organization. Efficiently managing the cross-functional relationships *within* key business processes can add tremendous value to the overall process.

AN OVERVIEW OF THE MODEL

In the course of our experiences working with businesses of all types and sizes, one consistent oversight has become evident: when we ask clients to produce documentation that describes "how work gets done," more often than not, they are unable to produce anything meaningful that describes the actual workflow within and between their departments.

First of all, it's essential that every key business process be documented. A simple diagram can provide an unambiguous and easy-to-understand picture that clarifies how all the elements associated with the process fit together. This makes it a valuable tool for verifying, in everyone's mind, how a particular job is done. It not only promotes consistency, but also eliminates confusion and clarifies understanding.

Having a formal method for documenting processes both within and among departments ensures well-designed and well-managed connections, communications, and handoffs among people and systems. The resulting "process map" clarifies not only the steps and who is responsible for each, but also where and how delays or mistakes are most likely to occur.

The definition of our process improvement model includes eight basic steps. This model has been developed and used successfully with clients in both public and private sectors, and colleges and universities. To effectively use the model, begin with a vision. That vision should identify the specific process goal. Typically, it includes descriptive verbs such as "improve," "increase," "reduce," or "eliminate." Once you've identified your goal, analyze each process associated with that goal using the following approach:

1. Document current processes
2. Evaluate the "As is" condition
3. Realign duties and responsibilities
4. Improve interdepartmental communications
5. Clarify staff responsibilities
6. Take advantage of technology
7. Prepare for change
8. Institutionalize process improvement

The Process Improvement Model

<u>Step One</u>: Document critical processes.

Unlike typical flowcharts, process maps illustrate the relationships among departments, people, and processes. By mapping a business process across various departments, you can clearly see the progression of activities and tasks that make up the operation. When done properly, this diagram should clearly identify:

- The *key steps* in each process
- The *interdependencies* of processes that connect offices or departments
- *Personnel* who carry out these processes
- Whether or not a documented *policy or procedure exists* for each step or task

While a variety of specialized software applications exist that simplify process mapping, we've found Microsoft Visio to be one of the easiest and most available tools around. By aligning the departments or people involved in horizontal or vertical *lanes*, you can create a useful workflow of the process. Points where process flows *"change lanes"* indicate handoffs from one person or department to another. You can find more information regarding process mapping, specifically the *"swim lane"* concept, in *Improving Performance*, an excellent text by Geary Rummler and Alan Brache (Jossey-Bass Publishers).

You can drill down processes into a series of subprocesses, depending upon the level of detail desired for the analysis. As a first pass, however, illustrate process maps at the highest level. If needed, any task or activity in the process can be isolated and reduced into a series of subprocesses or steps (i.e., its own process map) in order to analyze it more closely.

To accurately create this diagram, interview the staff engaged in the actual process to confirm both *the accuracy* of the diagram and *their understanding of the process*. This involves asking each participant a set of standardized questions such as:

- What initiates this process?
- From whom do you receive the request that signals the start of your efforts?
- What is your role or specific responsibilities in this process?
- Is there a written procedure that controls the way you perform this task or series of tasks?
- What defines the conclusion of your tasks or responsibilities in this process?
- What are the key performance criteria for your role in this process (timeliness, accuracy, or quality)?

<u>Step Two</u>: Evaluate the "as is" situation.

Documenting a process and confirming its accuracy with staff involved in the process leads to an "as is" or current description of the process. This "as is" diagram can be analyzed to find opportunities to improve processes. We've found that the most effective way to constructively evaluate this diagram is by bringing together a cross-functional team of stakeholders to review and recommend improvements to the existing process.

The team's directive should be to identify improvements that lead to improved quality of service, better throughput and response times, and lower processing costs. It should be comprised of both stakeholders involved in the process, as well as those with little or no knowledge of the process. The latter group brings a fresh, unbiased view of the process and is more apt to question the status quo or ask why.

In order to create an environment suitable to fostering an honest, nonthreatening critique of the "as is," we suggest leading the chosen team through Patrick Lencioni's *The Five Dysfunctions of a Team* (Jossey-Bass) utilizing their team building workbook. (Obtain copies of the workbook from www. tablegroup.com)

Solicit feedback from customers of the process (both internal and external). The customer experience aids in correlating those intangible factors that influence overall customer satisfaction. The team's resulting efforts should lead to the creation of a new process diagram that represents an improved process. Team members should also decide upon an appropriate measurement criteria and benchmarks in order to access the degree of improvement obtained at some future date. At the conclusion of this effort, management should recognize and reward team members for their participation and commitment to the effort.

Step Three: Realign duties and responsibilities accordingly.

Realigning processes will typically result in changes to existing job duties and responsibilities for those involved in the processes. This presents an excellent opportunity to more efficiently staff the departments involved in the process by: (1) shifting personnel to areas in need of added support and, (2) defining new responsibilities in accordance with the demands of the revised process.

Step Four: Improve interdepartmental communications.

A key objective of process improvement is to streamline and improve process activities both within and across department boundaries. Unfortunately, the "silo effect" creates barriers to effective collaboration across many departments. Each department has its own internal processes that, collectively, contribute to the overall effort. Typically, these internal processes are unknown outside of their specific departments. Start by educating employees. Build communications among departments that clearly define how their operations contribute to the overall process both internally and externally.

Step Five: Clarify staff responsibilities.

In our experience, untrained workers, undocumented work procedures, or a lack of skills necessary to perform a task can all lead to process inefficiencies. Be very clear and specific about responsibilities, job duties, and performance expectations.

Step Six: Take advantage of technology.

Documenting and analyzing processes can also provide an opportunity to identity ways to take greater advantage of technology. Electronic workflow systems have unique capabilities that allow for the automation of process-related tasks that staff may currently perform manually.

Step Seven: Prepare for change.

Finding opportunities to streamline and improve processes is easy. Making that change occur, however, is not. It should all begin with a compelling argument that clearly identifies why the process needs to change. Understanding the need for change helps pave the way for acceptance and buy-in. People and departments affected by process changes all have distinctly different characteristics, personalities, and motivations. Likewise, the prevailing "culture" has a strong impact upon the success of the change effort. We suggest reading John Kotter's classic article, "Leading Change" (Harvard Business Publishing).

When implementing process changes, forgo the broad, sweeping changes, and start small. Embrace the success of these incremental "wins" and build upon these accomplishments by moving forward gradually, with more change.

Step Eight: Institutionalize process improvement.

An ongoing, continuous effort ingrained in your business culture is the key to sustaining the process improvement "movement." Encourage employees to identify other key business processes for analysis and continually seek volunteers from all parts of the company to participate in this endeavor.

A Final Thought
On Processes

As portrayed by AMD in the story, the new reality of aggressive competition, changing world markets, and financial restructuring has forced businesses of all types to look "inward" to find ways to operate more efficiently and effectively. In addition, rising consumer expectations have created the need to consistently deliver exemplary customer service. In our experience, we've witnessed countless situations where tasks were simplified, eliminated, or combined to reduce the number of steps in a process. In each case, the results had a significant impact on the overall process, and ultimately the business itself. By adopting these concepts, you can realize improved throughput, fewer errors or delays, and, ultimately, greater profit potential.

So, as your organization's leader, embrace what Lucy has taught us; in most every case, it's not the people, it's the process.

Good luck in your endeavors.

About The Author

Walter T. Geer, Jr., is president and CEO of The CA Group in Boston. He has an extensive amount of experience helping clients solve complex business problems. His expertise includes information technology, strategic planning, business process reengineering, and technical leadership training. A graduate of Duke University, Mr. Geer gained this experience over a thirty-year period with such private sector Fortune 100 organizations as Philip Morris USA, Duracell, and GE, as well as in higher education where he served in senior administrative roles at the State University of New York, the Community College System of Massachusetts, and Harvard University. He lives in Boston with his wife, Wanda.

He can be reached at: walter.geer@thecagroup.org

www.ingramcontent.com/pod-product-compliance
Lightning Source LLC
Chambersburg PA
CBHW022109170526
45157CB00004B/1545